Vera Wang

A PASSION FOR BRIDAL AND LIFESTYLE DESIGN

By Diane Dakers

Crabtree Publishing Company
www.crabtreebooks.com

Crabtree Publishing Company

www.crabtreebooks.com

Author: Diane Dakers
Publishing plan research and development:
Sean Charlebois, Reagan Miller
Crabtree Publishing Company
Editors: Mark Sachner, Lynn Peppas
Proofreader: Wendy Scavuzzo
Indexer: Wendy Scavuzzo
Editorial director: Kathy Middleton
Photo researcher: Ruth Owen
Designer: Alix Wood
Production coordinator: Margaret Amy Salter
Production: Kim Richardson
Prepress technician: Margaret Amy Salter

Written, developed, and produced by
Water Buffalo Books

Publisher's note:
All quotations in this book come from original
sources and contain the spelling and grammatical
inconsistencies of the original text. The use of
such constructions is for the sake of preserving
the historical and literary accuracy of the sources.

Photographs and reproductions:
Alamy: page 37 (right)
Associated Press: page 60
Flickr (Creative Commons): page 65 (all); page 96
Getty Images: Phillip Massey: page 7; Loomis Dean: page 17; Clay Patrick
McBride: page 23; Frazer Harrison: page 31; Scott Wintrow: page 39; Scott
Gries: page 49; Rabbani and Solimene: page 57; Pascal Rondeau: page 59 Evan
Agostini: page 63; RJ Capak: page 69; Lawrence Lucier: page 73 Business Wire:
page 81; Scott Garfield: page 85
Public domain: page 37 (left); page 43
Shutterstock: front cover (background); page 1; page 4 (background); page 5;
page 9; page 10; page 13; page 15; page 18; page 19; page 20; page 21 (right);
page 22; page 26; page 27; page 29; page 33; page 38; page 42; page 45;
page 47; page 50; page 51 (all); page 52; page 53; page 54; page 55; page 62;
page 66; page 67; page 68 (all); page 71; page 74; page 76; page 82; page 83;
page 84; page 86; page 87 (all); page 89; page 90; page 94; page 95 (all);
page 97 (all); page 98; page 99; page 101; page 102 (all); page 103 (all)
Wikipedia (public domain): front cover (main); page 4 (inset); page 21;
page 35; page 91
Cover: Vera Wang is a fashion designer renowned for putting a modern
spin on classic style. Famous as a wedding-gown designer to the stars, she
has changed the entire wedding experience, from hairstyles and makeup to
invitations, and even the ceremony itself.

Library and Archives Canada Cataloguing in Publication

Dakers, Diane
　　　Vera Wang : a passion for bridal and lifestyle design / Diane
Dakers.

(Crabtree groundbreaker biographies)
Includes index.
Issued also in an electronic format.
ISBN 978-0-7787-2535-0 (bound).--ISBN 978-0-7787-2544-2 (pbk.)

　　　1. Wang, Vera--Juvenile literature. 2. Women fashion
designers--United States--Biography--Juvenile literature.
3. Fashion designers--United States--Biography--Juvenile
literature. 4. Fashion designers--New York (State)--New York--
Biography--Juvenile literature. 5. Wedding costume--United
States--Juvenile literature. I. Title. II. Series: Crabtree
groundbreaker biographies

TT505.W36D33 2011　　　j746.9'2092　　　C2010-903022-2

Library of Congress Cataloging-in-Publication Data

Dakers, Diane.
　Vera Wang : a passion for bridal and lifestyle design /
Diane Dakers.
　　　p. cm. -- (Crabtree groundbreaker biographies)
　Includes index.
　ISBN 978-0-7787-2544-2 (pbk. : alk. paper) --
ISBN 978-0-7787-2535-0 (reinforced library binding : alk.
paper) -- ISBN 978-1-4271-9467-1 (electronic (PDF))
　1. Wang, Vera--Juvenile literature. 2. Women fashion
designers--United States--Biography--Juvenile literature.
3. Fashion designers--United States--Biography--Juvenile
literature. 4. Fashion designers--New York (State)--New
York--Biography--Juvenile literature. 5. Wedding costume--
United States--Juvenile literature. I. Title. II. Series.

TT505.W36D35 2011
746.9'2092--dc22
[B]
　　　　　　　　　　　　　　　　　2010018043

Crabtree Publishing Company

www.crabtreebooks.com　　　1-800-387-7650

Printed in the USA/082010/BL20100723

**Published in
Canada
Crabtree Publishing**
616 Welland Ave.
St. Catharines, Ontario
L2M 5V6

**Published in
the United States
Crabtree Publishing**
PMB 59051
350 Fifth Avenue, 59th Floor
New York, New York 10118

**Published in
the United Kingdom
Crabtree Publishing**
Maritime House
Basin Road North, Hove
BN41 1WR

**Published in
Australia
Crabtree Publishing**
386 Mt. Alexander Rd.
Ascot Vale (Melbourne)
VIC 3032

Contents

Chapter 1
Designing Woman

At age 39, and soon to be married for the first time, Vera Wang was on the hunt for the perfect wedding gown. The year was 1989, a period in fashion history known for its ritzy glamour, exaggerated silhouettes, and fondness for doodads. For months, Vera scoured the shops and boutiques of New York City, where she found nothing but frothy, princess-style dresses designed with younger brides in mind. What she sought was something appropriate for a sophisticated older bride, something exquisite and elegant but simple and modern at the same time.

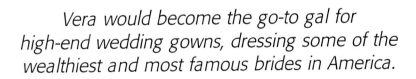

Vera would become the go-to gal for high-end wedding gowns, dressing some of the wealthiest and most famous brides in America.

Opposite: Vera Wang has taken the materials used to construct traditional wedding gowns and turned them into innovative creations for fashion-conscious brides.

Doing It Herself

Having been in the fashion business for more than 15 years—but never having designed a dress—Vera finally gave up the hunt for a store-bought dream dress and tried her hand at creating her own. She sketched and sketched until she came up with a look that pleased her. Then, with money from her parents, she hired an experienced dressmaker to sew the gown.

In June 1989, Vera Wang walked down the aisle wearing the beautifully beaded, sleek gown she'd designed, not knowing that this would be the first of thousands of dresses she would create in the coming years, revolutionizing the whole bridal business in the process.

Thanks to Vera, simplicity was suddenly elegant; women didn't need to be flashy to be noticed.

A Woman of Weddings— and Then Some

Over the next decade, Vera would become the go-to gal for high-end wedding gowns, dressing some of the wealthiest and most famous brides in America. In 1997, Vera designed a classic gown for Karenna Gore, daughter of then-Vice President Al Gore. Actress and former Miss

A bridal outfit from the Vera Wang 2006 Collection. The collection was launched at Brown Thomas, a store in Dublin, Ireland, specializing in some of the world's most exclusive designer fashions.

America Vanessa L. Williams wore Vera Wang for her 1999 wedding, as did Victoria Adams (now Victoria Beckham), better known as "Posh Spice" of the British girl group the Spice Girls.

Vera didn't just design gowns, though. Before long, she would change the entire wedding experience, offering her clients more than just a dress shop. She and her staff offered advice on everything: wedding invitations, flowers, hairstyles, make-up, even the ceremony itself. She recognized that women were busy—as she had been while she was planning her own wedding—and couldn't create their perfect wedding day alone. Because of Vera Wang, full-service bridal shops and planning services have become the norm for middle- and upper-income weddings.

*e been able
ajor artistic
n to bridal
g a fashion
to it."*

Wang

Simple and Elegant

From weddings, Vera branched out into evening-wear, dressing the likes of then-First Lady Hillary Rodham Clinton, actress Sharon Stone, and talk-show diva Oprah Winfrey. Glamorous actresses started wearing Vera Wang on the red carpets at the Emmy Awards, the Academy Awards, and the Grammy Awards, introducing the designer to television-watching American women.

Thanks to Vera, simplicity was suddenly elegant; women didn't need to be flashy to be noticed. Her design philosophy was as straightforward as was her clothing:

"For me, it's not about age—it's about comfort; it's about style," she said. "It's not about the clothing—it's about the way it's worn. ... There's an informality to the luxury."

With that point of view, Vera Wang changed the way American women dress for the big occasions in their lives. Soon, she would also change the way they decorated their homes, as she started stamping her name on silverware, stationery, linens, bedding, china, and crystal.

Within two decades, Vera Wang was a person, a clothing collection, a brand name, and a lifestyle. Women could dress head-to-toe in Vera Wang and decorate their homes, top-to-bottom in Vera Wang.

Vera Wang started her life as a little rich girl whose traditional Chinese parents never allowed her to take her posh existence for granted. She always had to work for what she wanted, however, first as a competitive figure skater whose goal was to reach the Olympics, then as a fashion and lifestyle designer who wanted to create a new look for American women.

Within two decades, Vera Wang was a person, a clothing collection, a brand name, and a lifestyle.

"I come from a wealthy family, but I'm a working girl from a working family," said Vera, who had no formal training in fashion design—just a dream and the business sense to make it a reality.

VERA WANG'S FASHION PHILOSOPHY

From the day she started in the bridal business, through her first ready-to-wear collection, to her discount line at Kohl's Department Stores, Vera Wang has always been true to herself and to her simple design philosophy. Her goal is to create comfortable clothing that celebrates women's bodies.

"Clothes are my passion and my knowledge," she said. "I've studied fashion from every angle—historically and critically, cerebrally and emotionally. Dressing celebrities gets you noticed. But I really do design for myself. And when my husband says I look sexy, I know I'm going to have a good night."

The secrets, she said, are things like flowing fabrics, a well-cut armhole or sleeve, and showing off a woman's best assets, while "sensuously draping fabric over less fabulous ones." Comfort, comfort, comfort is the key. "A woman is never sexier than when she is comfortable in her clothes," said Vera, who constantly sketches new designs no matter where she is—riding in cabs, watching TV, lying in bed. "She'll draw thousands of figures an inch-and-a-half high," said her husband, Arthur Becker. "I have nightmares that they're going to jump off the pad and tie me up."

A few of those sketches become designs-in-development, and even fewer of the designs-in-development make it into Vera's runway shows. Only the best of the best are good enough, a commitment to perfection that has made Vera so successful—that, and a belief that fashion design is her calling in life. "This is what I was meant to do. I was born for this."

THE BIG BUSINESS OF BRIDAL

Vera Wang has become the number one designer of high-end bridal wear in the world, but even she has just a small share in the multi-billion dollar wedding industry. Every year in the United States, about 2.1 million couples get married; in Canada, there are about 150,000 weddings every year; in China, more than 9 million.

While Vera Wang wedding dresses start at about $3,500 and can cost tens of thousands of dollars, the average American bride spends just $800 on her dress. Add to that the cost of catering, music, flowers, rings, bridal party attire, flowers, photography, and the honeymoon, and it's an expensive proposition. The average wedding in the United States sets the couple back more than $22,000. In Japan, weddings cost four times that amount!

A few more wedding facts:
- The number one month for weddings in North America is June, followed by August, July, or September, depending on the year.
- 99 per cent of newlywed couples take a honeymoon; the average honeymoon lasts one week.
- Destination weddings are becoming big business, with couples traveling away from their hometown—often to a tropical resort—to get married. The Halekulani Hotel, where a suite designed by Vera Wang is located, is on the list of top Hawaiian wedding destinations.
- Istanbul, Turkey, has more weddings every year than any other city in the world; Las Vegas is second.

A bride is fitted for her wedding gown in a scene that is repeated each year by millions of women the world over.

Chapter 2
Little Rich Girl

Given her privileged upbringing, one might think Vera Wang had everything handed to her on a silver platter—but that's not quite true. Vera still had to work hard for what she wanted in life, and her father didn't allow her to pursue her dream of becoming a fashion designer until she had all but given up on it.

A Good Start in Life

Vera Ellen Wang was born on June 27, 1949, and grew up on New York City's posh Upper East Side neighborhood. Her parents—father Cheng Ching Wang and mother Florence Wu— were born in Shanghai, China, but fled their homeland just after World War II to escape the

During the 1950s and 1960s, Florence often took her daughter to Paris, introducing the youngster to the finest fashion at runway shows and haute couture shops.

Chinese Communist revolution, a violent civil war. They immigrated to the United States, settling in New York City, where their two children, Vera and her younger brother, Kenneth, were born.

Once in the United States, Cheng Ching, the son of a Chinese general, started a company that produced medicinal drugs. He made his fortune distributing North American pharmaceuticals throughout Asia. The company, called U.S. Summit, continues today, with Kenneth as president. It employs 1,100 people in nine countries.

As her husband was building his international business, Vera's mother, the daughter of a wealthy Chinese politician, worked as a translator for the United Nations, the international organization headquartered in New York City. Together, the couple provided Vera and Kenneth with all the comforts that come with a posh Park Avenue existence.

The family frequently traveled internationally, often via luxury ocean liner, exposing Vera and her younger brother to different cultures and languages. Vera learned to speak Mandarin and French.

Today, Vera Wang calls her elegant mother her greatest fashion influence and cites those trips to Paris as where it all began.

In the 1950s and 1960s, Vera's mother introduced her to the world of fashion at runway shows and boutiques in Paris. Here, models show off Christian Dior's latest collection in a photo shoot in Paris in 1957.

To Paris with Mom

For Vera, one of the perks of growing up in such style was shopping in the world's fashion capitals with her glamorous mother. During the 1950s and 1960s, Florence often took her daughter to Paris, introducing the youngster to the finest fashion at runway shows and haute couture shops. Florence's favorite was the Yves St. Laurent boutique, where she bought expensive, made-to-order outfits. "We were one of St. Laurent's best clients," said Vera.

It was during these shopping trips that Vera's love for, and appreciation of, sophisticated fashion started to emerge. In Paris, she got a

For Christmas in 1956, Vera's parents gave her a pair of ice skates and, when her dad took her to the rink at Central Park to try them out, the youngster was instantly hooked.

close-up look at clothing created by some of the most popular designers of the day, and she got her first glimpses into the inner workings of the high fashion world that would one day be her domain. This was where she got her first inkling of where her future would lie. Today, Vera Wang calls her elegant mother her greatest fashion influence and cites those trips to Paris as where it all began.

THE WIDE WORLD OF FASHION

New York, London, Paris, and Milan are known as the fashion capitals of the world because of the number of designers who live and work there, the amount of money the fashion industry earns there, and the variety of clothing available there.

New York City has been the fashion hub of North America for more than a century. The city's Garment District or Fashion District may no longer be bustling with clothing manufacturers, as it once was, but it is still home to most of the top U.S. designers—including Vera Wang.

London, with its massive department stores, trendy boutiques, and amazing Portobello Market—a weekend flea market known for vintage and funky fashion stalls—is a shopper's heaven. Some of the hippest designers in the world, such as Stella McCartney and the late Alexander McQueen, hail from Britain's fashion center.

Paris, France, has been the heart of international fashion for more than 300 years. Worldwide trends start here, and designers like Coco Chanel, Yves Saint Laurent, and Christian Dior spent their careers here, creating looks that have been imitated around the world.

An industrial city in the north of Italy, Milan started to make its name as a fashion destination in the 1970s, when textile producers and designers began staging fashion shows to promote themselves. Most of the major Italian fashion houses, such as Valentino, Gucci, Versace, Armani, and Dolce & Gabbana, are now headquartered in Milan.

Back home in New York, Vera's hard-working parents taught their children to be disciplined, to strive for excellence in everything they did, and to take nothing for granted. At an exclusive all-girls school in Manhattan, young Vera learned to appreciate painting, design, architecture, and drama. She was a strong student who also excelled at physical activities. She studied ballet at the School of American Ballet and, at age seven, she discovered what would quickly become one of her true passions in life—figure skating.

Skater Girl

For Christmas in 1956, Vera's parents gave her a pair of ice skates and, when her dad took her to the rink at Central Park to try them out, the youngster was instantly hooked. At eight, she started taking private lessons at Madison Square Garden and, before long, she was entering local figure skating competitions. "Ice skating was the first love of [my] life," she said.

After winning her first regional championship at age 12, young Vera started taking her skating even more seriously.

As would become her lifelong pattern, Vera set her sights high—her goal was to reach the Olympic Games.

CELEBRATED SCHOOLGIRLS

From kindergarten through Grade 12, Vera Wang attended the Chapin School, an elite, Upper East Side, girls-only school. The school's motto, *Fortiter et Recte* (Bravely and Rightly) was created by the school's founder, Miss Maria Chapin, to encourage girls to stand up and be noticed. The motto must have worked, given some of the amazing women who graduated from the school: former First Lady Jacqueline Kennedy Onassis; actresses Sigourney Weaver, Stockard Channing, and Bebe Neuwirth; politician and author Christine Todd Whitman; author and pilot Anne Morrow Lindbergh; Queen Noor of Jordan; and socialites Ivanka Trump, Sunny von Bulow, and Lilly Pulitzer, who is also a fashion designer.

The Chapin School, in New York, boasts many well-known and successful graduates as well as a high placement rate in some of the nation's top colleges and universities.

The sport became her focus, with the discipline her parents had taught her serving her well. Through her childhood and teen years, Vera skated before school, and she skated after school:

"I thought nothing of waking up at four in the morning and rushing to the rink just to have ten minutes longer on the ice than my competitors. I had to sacrifice things, like a social life, to be a skater at 15. But I loved skating so much that it was worth everything to me."

As would become her lifelong pattern, Vera set her sights high—her goal was to reach the Olympic Games. In her late teens, she teamed up with a pairs partner, James Stuart, to compete at elite level events. In 1968 and 1969, the duo reached the U.S. National Figure Skating Championships, earning fifth place in the junior pairs competition in 1969. As a singles skater, though, Vera failed to make the cut and, after the fifth-place finish at the nationals, James chose to pursue a solo skating career. That left Vera without a skating partner and dashed her dreams of reaching the Olympics.

By this time, Vera was a student at the prestigious Sarah Lawrence College just north of New York City. She initially studied drama but soon realized that, as an Asian-American woman, her acting roles would be limited. After her Olympic dreams were shattered, she didn't really know what to do with her life, so she followed her father's wishes and enrolled in pre-med classes, with the intention of becoming a doctor.

FACES IN THE CROWD

The January 8, 1968, issue of *Sports Illustrated* featured 18-year-old Vera Wang in its weekly "Faces in the Crowd" segment, which turns the spotlight on up-and-coming teenage athletes:

"Vera Wang, a drama major at Sarah Lawrence College, hitched a last minute ride to the North Atlantic Figure Skating Championships ... and took the senior ladies title with a near-perfect performance."

Other athletes who have been honored as teenage "Faces in the Crowd" are golfer Jack Nicklaus (1957); tennis player Billie Jean King (1961); basketball star Earvin "Magic" Johnson (1977); sprinter Carl Lewis (1978); and figure skater Michelle Kwan (1993).

This photo of Vera, taken in 2006, appeared in Sports Illustrated *magazine to mark her earlier appearance, back in 1968, in the magazine's "Faces in the Crowd" section.*

She continued to skate on the side until her intense class schedule forced her to choose—school or skating? In the end, education won out, and 19-year-old Vera abandoned her dream of competitive skating once and for all, something she has since called "the major disappointment of my life." It wasn't long before she would give up on her goal of studying medicine, too.

Without her passion for figure skating to keep her going, Vera felt lost and overwhelmed. Within a year of quitting skating, she dropped out of school and moved to Paris to live with a figure-skating beau she'd met four years earlier.

A few months older than Vera, Patrick Pera was, by then, a four-time French figure skating champion who'd won a bronze medal in the 1968 Olympic Winter Games in Grenoble, France, and two bronze World Championship medals. (He would go on to win three more French championships, another Olympic bronze medal, and a World Championship silver medal before retiring from competitive skating.)

While in Paris, Vera enrolled in art history and languages courses at the University of Paris-Sorbonne, and when she broke up with Patrick Pera a year later, she returned to New York—and to Sarah Lawrence—to continue her art history studies there.

A Foot in the Fashion Door

During her third and fourth years at college, Vera had the option of taking classes in Europe. Naturally, her first choice for studying abroad was to return to Paris, where she continued pursuing her degree in art history while immersing herself in the art, architecture,

A FRENZIED WEEK OF FASHION

In the fashion world, Fashion Week is the busiest time. In a one-week period, dozens of designers show their latest collections in elaborate fashion shows that allow buyers and fashion journalists to see what's hot—and what's not—for the upcoming season.

Fashion Week happens twice a year. In the first quarter of the calendar year, Fashion Week showcases the designers' collections for the following fall and winter. Then, in the September to December period of each year, Fashion Week's focus is on the next spring and summer collections. This gives buyers plenty of time to place their orders and take delivery before the season arrives.

The biggest, most exciting Fashion Weeks happen in the four fashion capitals of the world—New York, London, Paris, and Milan—but Fashion Weeks now take place all over the world, in such far-flung cities as Agadir, Morocco; Minsk, Belarus; Rejkjavik, Iceland; Medellin, Colombia; Ennis, Ireland; and Lagos, Nigeria.

"For me, the idea that I could always do better, learn more, learn faster, is something that came from skating. But I carried that with me for the rest of my life."

Vera Wang

and history of the city. Of course, she was also immersed in the city's cutting-edge fashion scene. "When you're in Paris, you can't help but notice fashion," said Vera, who finally realized what would replace her passion for skating. "The only thing that I loved as much as skating were clothes," she said.

In the summer break between her third and fourth school years, Vera returned to New York and got her first fashion-related job—as a salesgirl at the Manhattan Yves Saint Laurent boutique, her mother's favorite. There, she met a customer, Frances Patiky Stein, who happened to be an editor at *Vogue* magazine. Vera so impressed Stein with her get-up-and-go, her passion for clothing, and her obvious eye for fashion that Stein told Vera to come see her after she graduated the following year if she wanted to work at *Vogue*.

Vera had other ideas upon graduation from Sarah Lawrence in 1971. She wanted to go to fashion school and study to be a designer. When she told her father, he refused to allow it. He wanted to make sure it was the right career choice for his daughter, that it was something she would be good at. "I want to see you get a job in fashion first," he said, and because Vera had been taught to honor her parents, she obeyed her dad's wishes and got in touch with Stein to take her up on her offer of a job at *Vogue*.

CONFUCIUS SAYS

Vera Wang may have been born, raised, and lived her whole life in New York, but her Chinese roots have always been deeply planted in her heart. Her parents, who grew up in China, instilled in Vera and her brother Kenneth the core values of their heritage.

"I'm totally Americanized, yet in many ways the feelings I have for people and the respect I have are inherently Chinese," she said.

Chinese culture is all about honor, respect, and ritual, based on the teachings of the ancient Chinese philosopher, Confucius, who believed each person should live to be the best he or she could be and treat others with great courtesy.

This includes such signs of respect as taking off your shoes before entering a house, bowing to an elder, writing a thank-you note, or bringing a gift when you visit someone's home.

For children, honoring their parents is a must, which is why Vera always followed her father's wishes. Self-discipline is another Confucian value, as are commitment to lifelong learning, hard work, and always striving to improve oneself. "In America we think anything is possible. The Chinese feel they have to work to deserve it," said Vera, who continues to practice traditional Chinese principles today.

Chapter 3
Vera In and Out of *Vogue*

The editor Vera Wang had met in the summer of 1970 was true to her word, and when Vera got in touch with her a year later, Frances Patiky Stein hired the 22-year-old college grad as an editorial assistant, someone who does general office work, runs errands, photocopies, and helps with anything else that's needed. Vera had finally arrived in the fashion world. She was working at *Vogue*, one of the most important fashion magazines in the world!

That first job at Vogue *may not have been glamorous—in fact, it was hard, often humdrum work—but Vera recognized it for the amazing learning opportunity it was.*

A Fashion Star Is Born

That first job at *Vogue* may not have been glamorous—in fact, it was hard, often humdrum work—but Vera recognized it for the amazing learning opportunity it was. "All I did my first year at *Vogue* was photocopy," she said. "But my father said to me: 'Keep doing it. You're learning the business from the ground up.' And he was right."

At age 23, Vera became the youngest editor in the magazine's history.

She soaked up everything she could about the fashion business. She learned about clothing and fashion photography, met designers and fashion writers, and experienced the nitty-gritty of the magazine business. "I would have done anything," said Vera, whose hard work didn't go unnoticed by her boss, veteran fashion editor Polly Allen Mellen.

"Vera had all the ingredients of a star," said Mellen. "You could tell that immediately."

All the energy, passion, and dedication Vera had previously thrown into her life as a competitive figure skater she now threw into her job as editorial assistant. "I was a great assistant, a true assistant. I mean, if something was left in my hands, it was done,

> "I ended up being exposed to more clothing at Vogue *than most people see in a lifetime. There couldn't have been a better education for me.*"

Vera Wang

Whether it's prepping for the runway or a photo shoot, paying close attention to every detail, including hair, make-up, and accessories, is critical to the entire "look" of the presentation. Here, Vera prepares a model backstage at the Vera Wang Spring 2006 fashion show, held in the fall of 2005 at Bryant Park in New York.

without even a concern," she said.

Vera put so much into her work, and impressed her bosses at *Vogue* to such a great degree, that, after just a year on the job, they promoted her to sittings editor. This job put her in charge of the magazine's fashion spreads, or photo layouts. At age 23, Vera became the youngest editor in the magazine's history. Her job was to decide which model would be featured in a photo spread, what the model would wear, how her hair and make-up would be done, how she would pose, and what background and props would be included.

"She used the perfection she learned as a skater to produce [photo] shoots with an ice-cool edge," wrote *Vogue* editors in an article about Vera many years later.

Vera worked with the world's top designers and photographers, learning everything she could about clothing and accessories, cut and color...

Thriving on Pressure

As demanding as Vera's role as editorial assistant had been, her new job was even more intense but, again, she proved she was up to the challenge—and again she was quickly promoted, this time to senior fashion editor.

She was just 25 years old. Said Vera about her job as a fashion editor:

"To be a fashion editor at Vogue, *which is about the highest you can attain in fashion magazine-land, there's nothing you haven't been exposed to, no conditions under which you haven't worked. You might be doing swimwear in January, or furs in July, with the makeup running and the hair limp and damp because the girl is sweating, but … if you don't come home with extraordinary pictures, you're in deep trouble."*

Vera worked long days, sometimes seven days a week, often coming home at two or three o'clock in the morning. During Fashion Week, her schedule was even more grueling. She would attend runway shows all day, then rush back to the office to look at photos, choose the outfits she wanted to highlight in the photo shoots, edit the photos, then put them all together in a magazine layout before going home to bed—only to repeat the process the next day and the day after that. "I lived at *Vogue*," she said.

As crazy as the lifestyle was, Vera thrived on the challenge of it. She worked with the world's top designers and photographers, learning everything she could about clothing and accessories, cut and color, what looked good on women's bodies, and how to make a living in the high-pressure, competitive fashion industry. She met the world's top designers—people like Ralph Lauren and Calvin Klein.

"It's like boot camp," she said. "But when you walk out of there your mind functions differently. You don't ever see the world in the same way. And for that I'll always be so incredibly grateful."

It was time for her to follow her heart into the side of fashion she truly craved—design.

After proving herself in New York, Vera was promoted to European editor of American *Vogue* in Paris. There, her position took her out of the studio, away from design and editorial, and into the world of cocktail parties and power lunches. It was quite a change:

> *"It was a little grand for me as a job. I like the gritty parts of fashion—the design, the studio, the pictures. I'm not really a girl who likes to go out to lunch or cocktails or store openings. I felt very removed. It wasn't just that I didn't like having lunch with Gianni Versace. It was just that I wanted to be a designer still. Very much."*

Vera didn't stay on the job in her beloved Paris very long, choosing instead to return to her previous *Vogue* job in New York City, where she would remain until 1987. At that

NOT TOO SURE THAT'S A COMPLIMENT...

Anna Wintour, *Vogue* magazine's longtime editor in chief, is said to be the inspiration for Meryl Streep's character, the demanding Miranda Priestly, in the 2006 Hollywood film *The Devil Wears Prada*.

Coincidentally, Anna Wintour once dated Vera's brother Kenneth.

Vogue *magazine's editor in chief, Anna Wintour, in the front row of a runway show in 2007.*

point, she had been at *Vogue* for 16 years, and when the position of editor in chief came up, she hoped it would be hers. Instead, the top job went to former British *Vogue* editor Anna Wintour, who has been in the position ever since.

At that moment, Vera knew she had gone as far as she could at *Vogue*. It was time to move on. It was time for her to follow her heart into the side of fashion she truly craved—design.

Love and Lauren

Before she left *Vogue*, Vera asked her father, again, for his permission to start her own design business but, again, he said he didn't

THE WORD ON FASHION

Vogue magazine, where Vera Wang spent 16 years of her career, may be one of the most significant fashion magazines out there today. But it certainly wasn't the first.

Hundreds of years ago, the only way one could find out what were the trends of the day was by seeing the style-makers—mostly members of royal families—in person. Some of the more thoughtful kings and queens kept their subjects updated on what was in and what was out by sending life-sized dolls, dressed in the latest styles, on tour around the country.

The first known fashion magazine, *Mercure Galant,* made its debut in France in 1672 and was read all over Europe. Almost 200 years later, in 1867, the first North American fashion magazine, *Harper's Bazar*—now *Harper's Bazaar*—hit the newsstands. It started as a weekly newspaper that brought news of European fashion to middle- and upper-class American women. In 1901, it became a monthly magazine.

Vogue got its start as a weekly publication in 1892, becoming a monthly magazine in 1973. Today, 18 different countries publish their own versions of *Vogue. Women's Wear Daily,* sometimes called "the bible of fashion," is a U.S. trade journal that was first published in 1910. It is known for dishing on the social lives of fashion designers, as well as their clothing.

The first all-Canadian fashion magazine, *Flare,* first hit the newsstands in 1979.

Left: The cover of Volume I, No. 49, of Harper's Bazar *(now* Harper's Bazaar), *dated October 3, 1862, shows an assortment of hairstyles of the day.*

Right: This 1929 issue of Vogue *magazine carries news of "Early Paris Fashions And Bridal Features."*

feel she was ready. He believed she needed more experience. After all, she may have had 16 years' experience at a fashion magazine, but she had yet to actually work in the design side of the business.

When she decided it was time to leave *Vogue*, Vera was offered—and accepted—a job with designer Geoffrey Beene, whose client list included several First Ladies and a number of movie stars. On the day Vera was to start at her new post, she got a call from another big-name designer, Ralph Lauren.

It turned out that he wanted to hire her as design director of accessories, and he was willing to pay her a lot of money for the privilege of having her. "He offered me four times [the salary] I'd ever had in my life, so I took [the job]," said Vera. "It was very hard on me because I idolized Geoffrey, and he never spoke to me again."

Finally, Vera was a designer. It wasn't her own clothing line yet but, still, she was designing. At Ralph Lauren, Vera was responsible for 13 different lines of women's accessories. She also designed sportswear and

The first time she saw a woman on the street carrying a handbag she'd designed, she could hardly contain her excitement.

lingerie. The first time she saw a woman on the street carrying a handbag she'd designed, she could hardly contain her excitement. She said she started "jumping up and down."

Life at the house of Lauren was much less hectic than Vera was used to, which meant that she had a bit of free time on her hands for the first time in years. Finally, she had time for a social life!

About seven years earlier, she had met businessman Arthur Becker at a tennis match. The couple had dated on and off back then but, because she wasn't ready for a serious relationship at the time, Vera broke up with him. "I have a career, I have places to go, people to see," she told him in 1980. They remained friends, though.

When Vera and Arthur ran into each other again in 1987, they started dating once more and, this time, Vera was ready to settle down. "I didn't wait for him, and he didn't wait for me, but as it turned out, years later, [when] we actually did meet again, it was really the right moment," she said.

Vera Wang and husband Arthur Becker arrive at the Whitney Gala 2004 at the Whitney Museum in New York City.

WHEN ARTHUR MET VERA

Vera has compared her friendship-dating-friendship-dating relationship with Arthur Becker to a 1989 movie. "We became friends, like in the movie *When Harry Met Sally.* Then we dated, then we decided we weren't even friends any more, then we became friends again, and in the end, we got married and had children."

Arthur didn't wait long before he asked Vera to marry him. Within a year, while the couple was on vacation in Hawaii, he popped the question. It was a spontaneous proposal, not exactly what Vera had expected. Still, she said yes. "Either she'd gotten smarter or I'd gotten more interesting," Arthur joked.

Not long after the casual Hawaiian proposal, Arthur asked for Vera's hand in marriage again, this time more formally and dramatically. One night, when they were out for dinner with good friends, Arthur arranged to have an engagement ring hidden in Vera's dessert. She wolfed the cake down so quickly, though, that he worried she'd swallowed it. "As he leaned over to examine what was left on my plate, my eye caught a slight glimmer of metal," said Vera. "At that instant, I knew." She saw the ring, hugged him, and said yes, again; she would love to marry him.

Immediately, the wedding planning—and the hunt for the perfect dress—was on. Little did Vera know that shopping for her wedding gown would change her life forever.

The Quest for the Dress

Vera and Arthur set their wedding date for June 1989 and, like most excited brides-to-be, Vera set out to find her dream dress. By this time, she was 39 years old and had a clear picture in her mind of how she wanted to look on her wedding day. "I'm very modern and sophisticated," she said. "I didn't want to look like the girl on top of the wedding cake."

She sought a gown that was lovely and elegant, sleek and romantic at the same time.

Since her dream dress didn't exist, Vera decided she would create it herself.

What she discovered, after three frustrating months of visiting every shop in the city, was that no such dress existed. All the gowns of the day were poufy and frilly off-the-shoulder numbers decorated with sequins and baubles— dresses that may have been perfect for a young woman in her 20s, but would look silly on a woman of 39. "There was one basic look at the time: 'frou-frou,'" said Vera, who eventually became so discouraged with her wedding dress hunt that she gave up. Since her dream dress didn't exist, she decided she would create it herself.

With money from her parents, Vera designed her own wedding gown, drawing on the knowledge she'd gained during her years in the fashion business. She hired a seamstress to sew the streamlined gown, which was glamorous and beaded—and heavy. The $10,000 dress weighed 25 pounds (11.3 kg).

On June 22, 1989, Vera Wang walked down the aisle in front of 400 guests, in the first of thousands of gowns she would design. Later, she said: "I didn't really like [the dress], but it was all even I knew about bridal at the time."

Vera and Arthur both wanted to have

NICE DAY FOR A WHITE WEDDING

Today, white—or ivory or cream—is the most common color for a wedding dress, but it wasn't always so. In fact, at one time, white was considered the appropriate color for mourning attire, and wedding dresses were brightly colored to reflect the bride's happy state.

Before the days of washing machines and dry cleaners, white dresses were hard to clean and impractical, and the idea of buying an elaborate dress for just one wearing was unheard of.

Britain's Queen Victoria changed that in 1840, when she wed her true love, Prince Albert. For the marriage ceremony, the young monarch wore a relatively simple white satin gown, with an 18-foot (5.5 m) train. The official wedding photo was published in America and all over Europe, allowing brides everywhere to see, and copy, the queen's look. Suddenly white wedding dresses were considered the height of fashion. They were also considered a status symbol because, if a bride could afford an impossible-to-clean white dress, it meant she was wealthy enough to buy a dress for only one wearing.

By the end of the 19th century, most upper-class women on both sides of the Atlantic Ocean followed suit, wearing white and ivory as they said their vows. By then, too, the white gown had come to symbolize purity and innocence. For middle- and working-class brides in North America, the white wedding trend didn't fully take hold until after the end of fabric rationing in World War II, but it has remained the most common look for weddings ever since.

An artist's representation of Queen Victoria and Prince Albert on their wedding day. Victoria's white wedding dress set a style standard for brides who wanted a once-in-a-lifetime gown for their wedding day.

children and, given that they were approaching middle age, they didn't want to waste any time. Immediately after their marriage, they started trying to get pregnant, but weren't successful. After six months, Vera started an intense program of daily fertility treatments and, when that, too, failed, she wondered if the stress of her job with Ralph Lauren was getting in the way.

"It was a difficult decision, but I couldn't try to get pregnant and carry the workload," she said. "We were determined to be parents." So, in 1989, after two years at Lauren, Vera quit her job with the man she still considers a mentor today, to focus her energies on becoming a mother.

Father Knows Best

Just when Vera thought she had her life and goals all sorted out, her father dropped a bombshell. He announced to his daughter that the time was finally right for her to start her own design business. "He said, 'Hey, why don't you start your own business?' I said, 'What, are you joking? I don't want to do it.' And he said, 'Now is the right time, because you don't want to do it. You won't be so emotional.'"

Then, another bombshell: "He said, 'Bridal.' I said, 'Are you kidding? I don't want to do bridal. It's a commodity. It's not fashion.'"

The more she thought about it, though, the more sense it made. Vera reflected on her own frustrations buying a wedding dress at 39 and realized her father had a good idea. There was a niche that wasn't being filled. Certainly there were other women like her who couldn't find a dress that suited their personalities:

"I thought I could bring fashion to weddings, and a different point of view, and do more modern dresses for girls who are more modern, and more romantic dresses for girls who are more romantic. I thought I could bring something new. I thought I could costume women for their weddings and suit their personalities."

With that thought, and $4 million borrowed from her father, Vera opened the two-story Vera Wang Bridal House Limited in the swanky Carlyle Hotel in Manhattan in September 1990.

LISTEN TO YOUR FATHER

One thing Vera Wang's dad taught her was to always be on the lookout for learning opportunities. He insisted that, no matter how much his daughter thought she knew, or how successful she became, she could always benefit from the people who'd gone before her. Today, she shares this advice with young people who want to become fashion designers: "Go work for somebody and get paid to learn. It's tempting to think you can go off and do your own thing, but there is so much to learn in ways you'd never know."

Chapter 4
Finally, a Designer ...

When Vera Wang first opened her bridal shop in Manhattan, she sold sophisticated and modern wedding gowns by international designers who appealed to her own personal taste—French designers Guy Laroche and Christian Dior, Canadian Arnold Scaasi and Venezuelan Carolina Herrera, among others. She wanted the boutique to cater to the New York elite, wealthy socialites, and celebrities. To help her run the business, Vera hired her friend Chet Hazzard, who had worked with designer Anne Klein, and other fashion houses in the past.

Booming Bridal Business

Some colleagues, like Ralph Lauren, truly believed in Vera and her potential in the bridal business. Others, including fellow designer Calvin Klein, were skeptical. "He thought I

The shop quickly became the go-to boutique for the bride-to-be with money to burn.

was crazy, saying that, when the bridal thing didn't work out, 'give me a call,'" said Vera.

It wasn't long before Vera proved the naysayers wrong. The shop quickly became the go-to boutique for the bride-to-be with money to burn. It didn't hurt that her former colleagues at *Vogue* ran a six-page magazine spread about Vera Wang Bridal House. After that, the customers poured in.

In her second year of business, Vera sold almost 1,000 wedding gowns, generating about $3 million, but she was still seriously in debt from starting up the luxurious shop. Instead of giving up, though, she started branching out, doing the one thing she'd always wanted to do—design her own fashions.

Over the next few years, she polished her skills and gradually started adding her own bridal creations to the showroom racks. "I thought of myself not as a bridal designer, but a fashion designer who happens to do white, ivory, nude," she said.

New York City's modern brides loved Vera's refined, uncluttered look. High-profile publications, including *The New York Times* and *People* magazine, took notice, giving her gowns rave reviews, and pretty much guaranteeing her success. Word spread quickly among the well-to-do of New England (the six northeasternmost states: Maine, Vermont, New Hampshire, Massachusetts, Rhode Island, and Connecticut).

The Vera Wang Bridal House didn't just sell wedding dresses. It sold a complete bridal service for busy career women, who were—as Vera had been when she was planning her own

> "I wanted to go into an area where I could make a real contribution. I think most of the great [fashion] houses that I admire have done that. Every house that I knew of started with one thing … For me, it would be wedding."
>
> Vera Wang

A model walks the runway during a Vera Wang bridal collection show in New York in 2007. This dress is a deep purple and, like so many of Vera's designs, challenges traditional notions about what a wedding dress "should" look like.

wedding—too busy to organize all the elements of the big day on their own:

"If I'm going to open a store, it's going to be about finding other Veras [who] are running around looking for special dresses, looking to have everything taken care of, because they have busy lives."

With her new way of approaching the bridal business, along with her fabulous designs, Vera had finally arrived among the ranks of serious designers.

Full-Service Bridal Care

True to her word, Vera and her staff offered advice on everything from jewelry to wedding-day hairdos and make-up, flowers, shoes, bridesmaids' dresses, even tips for the actual ceremony. She was the first designer to offer a wedding registry and a full-service website filled with information on the latest runway trends and wedding-planning ideas. Vera's goal was to create a whole new experience for the bride-to-be:

It can take four seamstresses more than six months to create one hand-embroidered, custom-made wedding gown designed by Vera Wang. The cost of such a gown would be about $20,000–$25,000, but it would include more than just the dress. As a full-service bridal business, Vera Wang Bridal House offers products and advice covering a whole range of wedding details, including flowers and accessories.

"For the price of one retail dress, you get a lot of attention plus all the accessories right there, and advice on everything, even flowers, and no consulting fee. I wanted to be exclusive by taste, not money. Small and caring. I look at every dress in the store. I had a whole glove line made up that didn't exist. And I was thinking wouldn't it be nice to take off your shoes, have a Diet Coke, and not be bride No. 5,076 for the month of June."

Her made-to-order customers got even more attention, usually from Vera herself, who would spend time with each bride-to-be, asking all kinds of questions—about the woman and the wedding—to help her create each individual's dream gown. "I always get involved in a wedding," said Vera. "Otherwise, I can't design the dress."

As a woman with seemingly endless energy, Vera managed to juggle family and business, transferring at least some of her creative passion to her children.

With her new way of approaching the bridal business, along with her fabulous designs, Vera had finally arrived among the ranks of serious designers. In 1994, the Council of Fashion

Tradition and Taste: A Balancing Act

The wedding business isn't easy for a designer, because a wedding gown isn't just a dress. It's an emotional symbol that often has to appeal to more people than just the bride, incorporating the opinions of all kinds of friends and relations. For a bridal wear designer like Vera Wang, creating the perfect dress can be an exercise in juggling tradition and taste, design and diplomacy.

For example, if every bride in a certain family has always worn great-grandma's lacy veil at her wedding, the designer has to tastefully incorporate this family heirloom into a look that satisfies the current bride-to-be. Vera is known for her knack for doing this, creatively combining all the elements to come up with a look that works—for everyone.

Over the years, she has also challenged a number of long-lived wedding traditions, including the notion of the white-only wedding day. She has been known to sew black velvet trim, a green bow, or a gold sash onto a dress. She offers wedding gowns in pale pinks, blues, and greens, bringing color back into a world that has been lily white for almost a century. Her signature design touch is to incorporate a stretchy, skin-toned fabric into the design to give the illusion of bare skin, while keeping the bride covered.

With such twists on tradition, Vera has transformed the bridal industry and has become the top wedding gown designer in the world today.

Designers of America (CFDA) invited her to join the organization. By then, she'd made her name as the woman who had modernized the wedding world. She'd dispensed with poufy skirts, billowy sleeves, and antique lace trim, replacing them with haute couture gowns for grown-ups. Her ready-to-wear dresses sold for $2,000 to $10,000, while the made-to-order, one-of-a-kind numbers were selling in the $15,000 to $30,000 price range. (Today, they can fetch even higher prices.)

Proving Herself to the Press

While her customers and others in the fashion world loved what Vera was doing design-wise, the fashion press wasn't so appreciative. Some saw the longtime *Vogue* editor as an industry insider who was getting special treatment and extra attention because of her previous job. Others believed she was just the spoiled daughter of a wealthy businessman, using family finances to get ahead.

Instead of lashing out at her critics, or giving up on her dream, Vera simply kept moving forward, as her family had taught her to do. "Nothing replaces hard work," she said, eventually silencing the critics with her continued success.

Within a few years, Vera Wang Bridal House was turning a profit, and Vera was ready to turn her attention to a new clothing line—and a new family.

In 1991, after giving up on the exhausting fertility treatments and trying to get pregnant, Vera and hubby Arthur Becker adopted a baby girl, whom they named Cecilia. In 1994, the

The CFDA

The Council of Fashion Designers of America (CFDA) is a not-for-profit trade association with more than 350 members, all from within the world of American fashion and accessory design. Admission to the CFDA is by invitation only. Every year, the organization honors outstanding designers at a glamorous awards ceremony. It also offers scholarships, education, and professional development opportunities to up-and-coming designers.

couple adopted their second child, another girl, named Josephine. "We weren't stuck on giving birth. We just wanted a family," said Vera.

If she thought running a business was demanding, Vera discovered that being a mom to two little girls was even harder. "Being a mother is the most challenging thing I've ever done," she said. "The biggest hurdle I face is lack of time."

As a woman with seemingly endless energy, though, Vera managed to juggle family and business, transferring at least some of her creative passion to her children. Like mother, like daughters, the girls would sit beside

Vera whenever she worked at home, scribbling their own designs on pads of paper.

Dressing for Success

With a thriving business, along with her desire to continually advance in her career, Vera felt the time was right to tackle a new design direction. The next logical step for her was eveningwear, a line she launched early in 1994 at such luxury New York City department stores as Saks Fifth Avenue, Barneys, and Neiman Marcus. Like her bridal designs, the new eveningwear collection combined the elegance of fine fabrics and elaborate beadwork with Vera's signature simplicity—and women loved it. "The customer embraced Vera's designs," said her business partner, Chet Hazzard. "She balanced fashion edginess with traditional elements."

Vera had always taken a hands-on approach with her business. With her garments now selling in multiple locations, she had to learn more about the operational side of the fashion industry so she could properly serve her newest customers, major department store buyers, and individual women. She was now exposed to the day-to-day details of running a multi-million-dollar company that many designers never see, gaining knowledge that would help further her success in the years to come. By the mid-1990s, Vera's business was bringing in about $10 million a year, thanks in large part to her new eveningwear collection.

Around the same time, the Vera Wang name spun into the international spotlight—literally—on the back of U.S. Olympic figure

Arthur Becker, Cecilia Becker, Vera Wang, and Josephine Becker pose for a family photo in 2006.

skater Nancy Kerrigan. In 1992, as a favor to Kerrigan's coach—a friend she used to skate with—Vera designed two costumes for the young skater. One was a lovely, delicate white outfit for Kerrigan's long program routine. The other was a neon yellow number with pale-pink

By the mid-1990s, Vera's clothes had also made it to the Academy Awards. In 1993, actress Sharon Stone was the first movie star to wear a Vera Wang design on the red carpet.

beadwork at the bustline, for the short program. That year, Kerrigan earned an Olympic bronze medal.

In 1994, Vera donated two costumes to Kerrigan's Olympic efforts. This time, for the short program, Kerrigan wore a snappy white dress with black velvet trim and sheer black sleeves valued at $9,300. For the long program, it was a $13,000 champagne-colored dress, hand-made with 20,000 Austrian crystals. Kerrigan's skating put her on the podium with a silver medal that year, and her costumes put Vera on the world stage. "I felt as though my life had come full circle," said Vera. "I didn't make it to that level of competition, but my clothes did."

VERA WANG ON ICE

Nancy Kerrigan wasn't the only U.S. figure skater to take Vera Wang to the Olympics. The designer also created costumes for Michelle Kwan, who won silver in the 1998 Olympics and bronze in 2002. "I dressed Michelle Kwan for about six years," said Vera. In 2009, Vera outfitted her first male skater, Evan Lysacek, for the World Championships, a competition he won wearing a sleek, black mock tuxedo. At the 2010 Olympic Winter Games in Vancouver, Lysacek skated to gold in two Vera Wang outfits—both all-black, one with jeweled snakes, the other with subtle sequins and feathers.

U.S. figure skater Nancy Kerrigan is shown at the 1994 Winter Olympics. Vera Wang designed two skating outfits for Kerrigan and donated them to the skater. Their combined value was estimated at over $22,000.

Designing for figure skaters, such as Michelle Kwan, "is much more complicated than you'd think," says Vera Wang. "You have to make sure [the skater] can move and bend and all the pieces stay anchored on." Fortunately, Vera has enough experience as an international-caliber skater that she understands the athletes' needs, allowing her to create costumes that are fashionable and functional.

COSTUME DESIGN 101

In 2009, Vera Wang was inducted into the U.S. Figure Skating Hall of Fame for her contributions to costume design. Here are some of her tips about successfully designing figure skating outfits that are both durable and stylish:

Choosing the Material—Weight and flexibility of the fabric are Vera's first considerations. "It has to have a certain finish or allure, properties that make [the skater] light and weightless."

Sewing—Seams are triple-sewed to make sure they don't tear. "You wouldn't want someone to lose Olympic gold because their sleeve ripped off."

Decoration—All adornments have to be tightly secured. "My worst nightmare is that something goes wrong with the costume that makes [the skater] fall or get distracted."

The Look—A figure skating costume has to look like formal wear but function like sportswear. "It's like creating the nightmare combination of an evening gown and a bathing suit! If a skater is competing for the Olympics, and they're not happy with the costume, you have taken some of the joy out of their performance."

By the mid-1990s, Vera's clothes had also made it to the Academy Awards. In 1993, actress Sharon Stone was the first movie star to wear a Vera Wang design on the red carpet—a stunning, champagne-colored halter dress. A year later, actresses Holly Hunter and Marisa Tomei followed suit. In 1995, it was Alicia Silverstone and Mare Winningham who wore Vera Wang to the Oscars.

By 1998, when Stone appeared at the Oscars wearing a glamorous lavender Vera Wang skirt topped with a man's crisp white shirt, Wang ensembles had become regulars with the Hollywood who's-who, drawing international attention to the designer and her style. "I love the glamour of dressing a star," said Vera. "I still get excited when I see my clothes at the Oscars."

From the celebrities' perspective, one of the best things about Vera is her discretion, keeping the details of their lives to herself—"I know everything about all of them and can't say a word," Vera once said.

Barbies, Branding, and a Book

Vera Wang couldn't have asked for better advertising than Hollywood celebrities wearing her made-to-order gowns on the red carpet and skaters modeling her designs on ice rinks around the world. Still, the designer didn't feel that she could relax in the ultra-competitive world of fashion.

"Every night, she comes home and tells me she's failing," said husband Arthur Becker in the late 1990s.

Sharon Stone and then-husband Phil Bronstein arrive at the 1998 Academy Awards. Stone's ensemble—a Vera Wang skirt and man's dress shirt—is considered to be one of the most memorable red carpet outfits in Oscar history.

CELEBRITY STYLE

Vera Wang has dressed the best in Hollywood, her outfits having been worn on red carpets and along the wedding aisles of the rich and famous since the mid-1990s. Her clientele list reads like a who's-who of Hollywood royalty. Stars like Goldie Hawn, Meg Ryan, Whoopi Goldberg, Helen Hunt, Cate Blanchett, Alicia Silverstone, Halle Berry, Rachel Weisz, and Charlize Theron have all worn Wang for their moments in the spotlight.

Mariah Carey was one of the first celebs to wear a Vera Wang wedding gown—a spectacular Cinderella-style dress with a 27-foot (8.2 m) train for her 1993 wedding to music executive Tommy Mottola. Others who have been wed in Vera's creations are Jennifer Lopez, Jessica Simpson, Avril Lavigne, Vanessa L. Williams, Victoria Beckham, Jennifer Garner, Holly Hunter, and Uma Thurman.

Even Barbie has worn a Vera Wang wedding dress. In 1998, the designer created an ivory satin gown trimmed in black velvet, with a blue flower at the waist, and pearly buttons down the back for the lucky doll.

With her attention to detail, Vera is often more nervous than the bride on the big day. When Sharon Stone married newspaper editor Phil Bronstein in 1998, the designer worried that her pale pink dress wasn't fitting properly. "We were literally sewing it onto Sharon's body the minute before she was going to come down the aisle," said Vera. "Sharon was cool. She had to calm me down."

Dressed in a Vera Wang gown, actress Rachel Weisz arrives at the 2007 79th Annual Academy Awards.

America Ferrera arrives at the 2009 Screen Actors Guild Awards in a dress by Vera Wang. Ferrera, the star of the TV series Ugly Betty, was a nominee for Outstanding Performance by a Female Actor in a Comedy Series.

For the designer, whom Sharon Stone once called "compulsively creative," her constant worry over the success of her business pushed her to work even harder, always coming up with new ideas, new clothing lines, and new directions. "I feel pressure, which I don't think I felt as much in earlier years," said Vera at the time. "As you become more high profile, you have more to lose."

Far from losing ground, Vera's drive propelled her name and her company to soaring heights throughout the 1990s. To keep up with the demand for her dresses, she opened in-store boutiques in luxury department stores in other U.S. cities, including Chicago, Los Angeles, Nashville, and Seattle. She opened her second stand-alone bridal boutique in Washington, D.C., in 1996, the same year she introduced her first line of bridesmaid dresses.

In 1997, she teamed up with Italian shoe company Rossimoda to create a line of dressy Vera Wang shoes, to go with her evening and bridal wear. "It's about the whole picture, not just the dress," she said. "The wrong veil can ruin the look, and so can the wrong pair of shoes." The deal with Rossimoda was the first in a series of licensing agreements Vera would enter into over the years.

In April 1998, Vera staged her first-ever New York fashion show, introducing her evening gowns to her fans, the fashion press, and prospective store buyers.

Licensing means Vera agrees to let another company manufacture a product—in this case, a pair of shoes—with her name on it. The company, in turn, agrees to give the designer a share of the money it makes selling that product.

In April 1998, Vera staged her first-ever New York fashion show, introducing her evening gowns to her fans, the fashion press, and prospective store buyers. The event was a big hit and led to even more success for the designer, who opened a boutique in Saks Fifth Avenue in San Francisco, the only shop other than her original Manhattan location to sell both the bridal and evening gown lines.

Later that year, Vera Wang Bride Barbie made her debut, with a second Barbie—a red-haired movie star dressed for the red carpet in a purple satin gown—appearing the following year as part of the Designer Barbie series. Also in 1999, Vera set up a second licensing agreement, this time teaming up with a company that would make leather and fur garments in her name.

As Vera entered the 21st century, her company employed more than 200 people and earned more than $20 million a year. In some ways, though, after 10 years in the bridal and evening gown business, Vera Wang was just getting started. With shoes, leather, and furs now bearing her name, she had gotten her first taste of being Vera Wang, the brand, not just Vera Wang, the wedding dress designer.

In the next few years, her drive, creativity, and business savvy would take her a step further, helping her become Vera Wang, the household name.

In 1999, a second Vera Wang Barbie made her appearance. Dressed in a purple outfit and ready for the red carpet, she was part of the Designer Barbie series of dolls.

Chapter 5
Vera Wang in the 21st Century

By the turn of the century, Vera Wang had made her name as the go-to designer for luxury wedding gowns and evening dresses, but she realized she had nothing for the average North American—the woman who couldn't afford a $1,000 party dress or a $5,000 wedding gown. Over the next few years, Vera set out to create a world in which everyone could own a Vera Wang.

All for Wang, and Wang for All

The first thing she did was put her years of wedding expertise into a book. *Vera Wang on Weddings*, published in October 2001, walks readers through the entire marriage cycle, from proposal to honeymoon. Filled with glossy

... [S]he was selling more than 10,000 custom-made wedding gowns every year.

photos, it includes advice, stories, and details to consider when planning the big day. The $65 book was Vera's way of reaching the women who loved her wedding gown designs but didn't have the money to buy one. "If they can't afford the dress, they can still take a part of me with them," she said.

By the following spring, women could take her with them in a different way—by spraying on her perfume. Vera launched her first signature fragrance, called Vera Wang Eau de Parfum, at Sak's Fifth Avenue in New York City on Valentine's Day, February 14, 2002. It sold so well, and so quickly, that it broke the record for highest sales of a new perfume at Sak's.

A mixture of rose, calla lily, and mandarin flower, with a touch of lotus, gardenia, iris, and musk, the fragrance was designed to add to the romance of a bride's engagement, wedding, and honeymoon period. Of course, the hope was that if a woman started wearing the Eau de Parfum for her wedding, she would continue to wear it—and buy it—for years to come.

The fragrance line also included bath and body products, such as lotions, powder, and soap. At $20 to $45 for the bath products, and perfume starting at $65, many women could suddenly afford a Vera Wang product.

Vera Wang Eau de Parfum won a 2003 FiFi Award for best new fragrance. Presented annually by the Fragrance Foundation, the FiFi Awards celebrate the best in the world in the fragrance industry, and are considered the Academy Awards of the perfume biz.

Within months of the fragrance launch, Vera ...led sunglasses and frames for prescription ...glasses to her inventory. "Vera never stops ...h the dress," said Chet Hazzard. "She is ...king at the entire woman and, for her, this ...he completion of the look." Now Vera Wang fans could wear the designer's name from head to toe.

Next up for the designer was the unveiling of the Vera Wang China and Crystal Collection. Within six months of its launch, three of the china patterns had already made the top 10 best-seller list at bridal registries across the United States.

Moving into the New Millennium

The first two years of the 21st century were busy times for Vera. During this period, she expanded and ...ovated her original Manhattan shop, which ...v sold bridesmaids' dresses, footwear, and ...er wedding accessories. She opened dozens ...ew boutiques across America. She teamed ...with a bigger-name partner for her line of ...es—Stuart Weitzman. And, to top it off, she ...s selling more than 10,000 custom-made ...dding gowns every year.

...lost significantly, in 2002, Vera Wang ...sented her first line of ready-to-wear

A REMINDER OF A SPECIAL DAY

A study by Unilever, the company that made Vera Wang Eau de Parfum on Vera's behalf, showed that 70 percent of women in the 25- to 35-year-old range continued to wear the scent they wore at their wedding, because it reminded them of that special day.

clothing. She created modern, affordable sportswear and funky separates—tops, pants, and skirts—allowing women of average income to wear the Wang label.

Vera's new creations may have been less expensive than her bridal and eveningwear, but they still featured her signature design elements. Like her luxury garments, the ready-to-wear fashions were comfortable but elegant, sophisticated, and hip at the same time. She used a variety of fabrics and textures, and unusual shapes and color combinations in each ensemble. "These are clothes that I would wear," said Vera, who is often spotted wearing her favorite look—simple black leggings with unusual tops.

After ten years as a bridal designer, and almost 30 years since she'd first asked her father for his support in starting a fashion design business, Vera had finally realized her dream. She was, at last, designing a full line of clothing for a cross-section of women. "It is horrible to say, but I was stigmatized by being a bridal designer for a long time," she said. "I am amazed I have been able to move beyond it. I had really all but given up trying, but I did it because it was my lifelong dream."

Dollars for the Dream

Designing a full range of clothing for a full range of women may have been Vera's dream—but it was an expensive dream. Creating ready-

Vera had finally realized her dream. She was, at last, designing a full line of clothing for a cross-section of women.

to-wear collections is costly, because the designer must supply a store with an assortment of styles in a variety of sizes and color choices, and there is no guarantee the clothing will sell. Unlike a made-to-order dress that the customer pays for as it is being made, ready-to-wear clothing must be financed by the designer before it can be manufactured and sold.

Knowing she needed money to keep a ready-to-wear business going, Vera began lending her name to more and more products. In 2003, she launched a line of jewelry, which made its debut on the red carpet when actress Sarah Jessica Parker wore some of the pieces to the Emmy Awards. In 2004, Vera launched her Silver and Gifts Collection—cutlery, cocktail accessories, and gift items. A new fragrance, Vera Wang for Men, also hit the stores in 2004.

Soon, Vera Wang products—other than clothing—were bringing in about $200 million a year. "The very fact that people could buy my products made me feel real," Vera said. "It is that amount of money from licensing that allowed me to invest something back into the clothing."

Whenever her ready-to-wear line lost money, she knew her fragrance or china or jewelry lines would cover the losses. "I've never had that kind of money before," she said.

By this time, Vera Wang was successful beyond what she'd ever thought she'd be, earning more money than she ever expected she could. Still, she continued to develop

"Vera loves clothes. Vera loves clothes beyond loving clothes; she loves everything that has to do with clothes. This is not a make-believe love here; it's the real thing. Anything that has happened to Vera is a fallout of this love. It's her only agenda. So she is going to present you clothes in an extremely loving manner: beautiful clothes in the most beautiful way possible."

Paul Cavaco, creative director, *Allure* magazine

her business, continually reaching for the stars, as her father had taught her to do as a child. "There isn't room in fashion today for little businesses," she said. "It's a question of survival ... It's grow or die, as they say on Wall Street."

A Time of Loss

From a business perspective, the middle years of the first decade of the century were a time of great reward for Vera. Personally, though, it was a time of great loss. Within three years, she lost three of the people closest to her.

First, her lovely mother—the woman whose elegance and sophistication had given Vera her early passion for fashion—died in January 2004. Just over a year later, her longtime friend and business partner, Chet Hazzard, also passed away at age 50. Sadly, the day he died could have been one of Vera's happiest, because it was the same day she was nominated for a Council of Fashion Designers of America (CFDA) Award.

Eighteen months later, in September 2006, the man who had given his daughter his blessing—and his money—to become a fashion designer, Vera's beloved father, died. Later that same day, Vera honored her dad by unveiling her spring 2007 collection, as planned, in an emotional runway show.

As sad as these years were, they were also a time of great achievement for Vera. Early in 2005, she opened her first bridal store in her parents' homeland of China, at the Pudong Shangri-La Hotel in Shanghai. That spring, when major New York department store

ON THE SIDELINES, BUT IN A GOOD WAY

In 2003, Vera Wang designed new uniforms for the Philadelphia Eagles cheering squad. The outfits made their television debut on *Monday Night Football* in September of that year.

RETURNING TO HER ROOTS

In 2005, Vera Wang opened her first store in Shanghai, one of China's largest cities, and later that year, she became the first Chinese American to be named International Fashion Designer of the Year at the China Fashion Awards. With her father, she went to Shanghai to accept the award and to visit the city where her parents had once lived. Cheng Ching Wang showed his daughter a modern culture, but one that still embraced its centuries-old traditions.

"This is a very big deal for me emotionally," she said of the experience. "It really is my roots."

SUITE VERA

A wealthy bride who slips into a Vera Wang gown for her wedding might also want to slip into the Vera Wang Suite for a Hawaiian honeymoon. In 2005, Vera designed every detail of a luxurious second-floor suite overlooking Waikiki Beach at the Halekulani Hotel. It is for "a very worldly, sophisticated consumer where quality, taste, originality, and comfort are the most important criteria," said a hotel executive.

For Vera, whose husband Arthur Becker first proposed to her in Hawaii, the location was especially significant. Her goal in designing the suite was to create "a sensual, sophisticated world in which every last detail is attended to and carefully considered."

The Vera Wang Suite, which rents for $5,500 a night, is furnished with Vera Wang linens, pillows, china, crystal, and silverware, along with Hawaiian and Asian items hand-picked by the designer. The bathroom is stocked with Vera Wang soaps, shampoo, lotions, and perfumes. The in-room menu features some of her favorite foods and favorite movies. The hotel lobby houses a Vera Wang boutique that sells beachwear, sunglasses, and gift items.

Vera isn't the only designer whose name is stamped on a hotel room. Her mentor, Ralph Lauren, has designed hotel rooms in Jamaica. An Oscar de la Renta room can be rented in the Dominican Republic, Todd Oldham is in Miami, and Christian Lacroix has adorned rooms in France. The houses of Armani, Versace, Moschino, and Ferragamo are also in the hotel business.

The Vera Wang Suite made its debut in 2005. Overlooking Waikiki Beach in Hawaii from the second floor of the Halekulani Hotel, the suite was billed as "the world's most romantic luxury suite." Shown here: the living room of the suite, where Vera Wang has designed every detail and hand-picked every piece of furniture as well as the china, crystal, linens, silverware, and even DVDs and menu items.

Bergdorf Goodman installed a Vera Wang salon, the designer felt she'd truly arrived in the world of ready-to-wear. That same year, she won the CFDA Award for Women's Wear Designer of the Year, one of the most prestigious awards in American fashion, and she took on her first-ever commercial interior design project and created the Vera Wang Suite at a swanky Hawaiian hotel.

By the end of 2005, products bearing the Vera Wang name were bringing in about $300 million a year, and the business was showing no signs of slowing down.

Vera is a night owl who stays up late and sleeps in late before hitting the ground running every day.

Vera Wang at Home

Vera constantly struggled to find a balance between her family life and her work commitments but, somehow, no matter how busy she was, she always managed to find some precious time for her young daughters. The girls coped well with their mom's international fame and dedication to her work. "They have a good sense of humor—they have to," said Vera.

Like their mother, Cecilia and Josephine

have both attended the Chapin School.
Cecilia has graduated and is now attending
the University of Pennsylvania. Also like their
mother, both girls have excellent taste in fashion.
"I love the way they dress. So modern," said Vera,
who has been known to ask for her daughters'
help in keeping up with the latest fashion trends.

During her down time, Vera likes to spend
time quietly at home with Arthur and the girls,
eating fast food and watching TV. She might
help Josephine with her homework and do a
few chores around the house before settling
back in to work late into the night. Vera is
a night owl who stays up late and sleeps
in late before hitting the ground running
every day.

She loves to read, golf, and travel the
world, sometimes combining a business trip
with a personal vacation. Of course, Vera
also loves to shop for designer clothing:

*"I love owning, wearing, or studying
the designer who does something
the best. If you don't know
who does what best, it's very
hard to know if what you're
doing is good."*

Vera's marriage to Arthur is solid,
something she gives him much credit
for. "My husband's a great, great
partner—as a husband and a father,"
she said. "He's also a workaholic.
If I didn't have somebody who was
really into his own profession,
there's no way he'd put up with

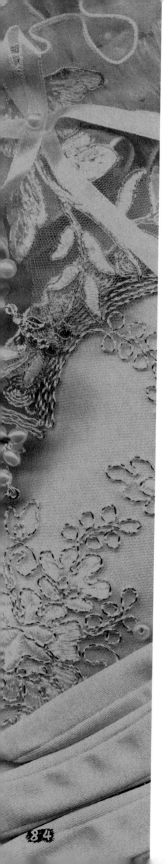

a wife like me."

Arthur's one wish is that his wife would understand just how talented she is and relax with it a bit. "That's the thing about people who strive," he said. "They just keep striving. I'd like her to have the sense of satisfaction, of pleasure, of being at ease with herself."

Today, the Wang-Becker family lives in a multi-million dollar apartment on Park Avenue, on New York City's Upper East Side—the same neighborhood where Vera grew up. In fact, she and Arthur bought their current apartment from her brother Kenneth in 2007 for $23.1 million. The apartment has an enormous walk-in closet to accommodate Vera's equally enormous clothing collection.

The family also has a beach house in Southampton, Long Island, just east of Manhattan, where they spend weekends and short vacations; a home in Palm Beach, Florida; and a home at Pound Ridge, 45 minutes northeast of New York City. Vera helped design the stone house, where her father lived before his death in 2007. It's the place Vera goes when

The apartment has an enormous walk-in closet to accommodate Vera's equally enormous clothing collection.

VERA WANG ON TV

For years, Vera Wang has dressed movie stars and television personalities but, in the last few years, she's become one herself. In 2006, she served as a guest judge on the fashion reality TV show *Project Runway* and in 2008 participated in an episode of *The Apprentice*.

Other TV shows she's done (always playing herself):
- *Sex and the City* (2004)
- *Ugly Betty* (2007)
- *Keeping Up with the Kardashians* (2009)

On the big screen, Vera has been featured in these movies:
- *First Daughter* (2004)
- *Sex and the City* (2008)
- *The September Issue* (2009)

Vera Wang (foreground) and Victoria Beckham (background) appeared as themselves in an episode of the TV comedy Ugly Betty. *Airing in November 2007, the episode concerned the role that both style celebrities played in the wedding of the villainous Wilhelmina Slater, played by Vanessa L. Williams (foreground, in white).*

she needs to truly escape the chaos of her life in New York. "I never relax in Manhattan," she said. "Up here, [I can] finally take a breath. A weekend here is as valuable as a month somewhere else."

The house is on a lake where the family swims, boats, and fishes in summer, and ice skates in winter, a passion Vera has passed on to her daughters.

Meanwhile, Back at Work ...

As the first decade of the 21st century wound down, Vera Wang continued to challenge herself and to move into new markets. She opened more boutiques across the United States; she expanded her bridal business to include a slightly less expensive line—with gowns starting at about $3,000. She also introduced Vera Wang's Lavender Label Collection, another ready-to-wear collection of tops, pants, and separates, this one for her upper-income clientele.

Before long, Vera launched a third ready-to-wear clothing collection, this one aimed at the opposite end of the spectrum—a value-priced line sold at Kohl's, a chain of value-priced department stores. Her critics said the move had the potential to ruin the Vera Wang name.

ANOTHER AWARD

In 2006, Vera Wang was awarded the Andre Leon Talley Lifetime Achievement Award from the Savannah College of Art and Design. Andre Leon Talley, who has been a significant player in the fashion world for more than 25 years, spent the bulk of his career working at *Vogue*. Today, he is probably best known as a judge on the TV reality series *America's Next Top Model*.

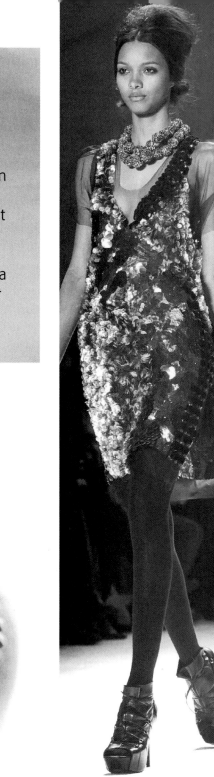

Chapter 6
New Directions

After years of catering to wealthy socialites and the Hollywood who's-who, Vera Wang had already taken one step toward outfitting average-income American women in 2002, when she launched her first ready-to-wear line. Five years later, she took a step even further down the price scale—and further up in her efforts to reach the nation's working women—when she linked up with Kohl's Department Stores, a chain known as a bargain-hunter's heaven.

Simply Vera

Some fashion insiders called Vera's new line "cheap chic," or "democratized style," but her critics called it a big mistake. They feared the

In 2007, with hundreds of stores across America, Kohl's was ready to follow in the footsteps of those same competitors and launch an affordable designer fashion collection.

discount line would ruin the Vera Wang reputation for luxury, sophistication, and distinctiveness.

In 1946, Max Kohl, a Jewish immigrant from Poland who had run conventional grocery stores, opened his first supermarket in Milwaukee. Before long, Kohl's was the largest supermarket chain in Wisconsin. In 1962, Kohl opened a department store that became the flagship store for the large chain of department stores that still carry his name.

Coincidentally, that was the same year Wal-Mart, Target, and Kmart—Kohl's main competitors in the United States today—also opened for business. In 2007, with hundreds of stores across America, Kohl's was ready to follow in the footsteps of those same competitors and launch an affordable designer fashion collection.

Kmart was already successful with its Martha Stewart home fashions, and Target

Vera Wang in 20

was doing well with a budget collection by designer Isaac Mizrahi. Wal-Mart, on the other hand, had failed in its efforts to move into discount designer clothing, choosing to team up with lesser-known designer Mark Eisen rather than a well-known name. In the 1980s, high-end stores dropped legendary designer Halston like a hot potato when he chose to sell a lower-end line at the more mainstream J.C. Penney, a move that dealt a serious blow to the Halston empire.

Not surprisingly then, fashion insiders were wary of a union between Kohl's, which bills itself as "value-oriented," and Vera Wang, whose website says her collections "are positioned at the highest end of the luxury market." They thought it could spell trouble for Vera's business.

Kohl's was looking to reinvent itself by giving its customers more than just value—the store wanted to add a dash of flash to its image. At the same time, Vera was looking for a way to bring in more money and reach more people.

Instead of listening to the worrywarts who thought she was making a mistake, Vera trusted her instincts and her understanding of what women wanted to wear.

"This is ... about keeping my business going so I can continue to do what I love most," she said.

Making the Fit a Good One

After a year of negotiating, conducting research, and surveying Kohl's customers about what they would buy and how much they would pay for it, both parties felt the marriage of the two businesses was worth the gamble. Instead of listening to the worry-warts who thought she was making a mistake, Vera trusted her instincts and her understanding of what women wanted to wear. "Let's be realistic, how many people are buying a $2,000 skirt?" she said. "I love to design things that people can actually buy." Vera believed the success of Mizrahi at Target showed there was an appetite for another low-priced line by a high-end designer, and she went for it.

In September 2007, the new line, called Simply Vera—Vera Wang, made its debut at Kohl's, and it has been a success ever since. The collection features separates and dresses,

"I love clothes. They're a very wonderful outlet for creativity, to challenge yourself to create an image and change how things work. Women are real works of art, and I try to remember that that's what makes it worthwhile, that it's not just about making money and seeing how big the distribution can be. It's about pleasure, giving it to other people, and getting it."

Vera Wang

along with sunglasses, bags, hosiery, pajamas, and underwear, with about 20 new pieces added every month.

Of course, there have been some differences of opinion between budget-minded Kohl's and the fashion-forward designer in terms of what the Simply Vera line should include. For example, Vera once wanted to put a gold brocade skirt in the collection. A Kohl's rep said: "Yikes, Vera. This is for nearly 1,000 stores. You can't just start throwing things [like that] in." In the end, they compromised, and the skirt made it into the Kohl's stores in small quantities. The skirt looked just like the $890 one featured in Vera's ready-to-wear collection at Bergdorf Goodman that year. The Kohl's version cost just $68.

Consumers were no longer looking for long-wearing fashion; they wanted cheap chic designed to get them through a season or two before being replaced.

Some women felt the brocade skirt and other Simply Vera items were too fancy for their day-to-day lives. "This is too over-the-top," said one customer of the collection. "This is not 'mom'

Is There Anything This Designer Doesn't Do?

In 2006, Vera Wang got into the bed business when she linked up with mattress-maker Serta. Today, the Vera Wang by Serta Collection includes such mattresses as the Signature Bridal Bed, which once took a lead role on the TV show *The Apprentice*; the Floral Bed, featuring flowery embroidery and organic cotton; and the Sweetheart Bed, with its triple-heart pattern.

Now you can sleep in a Vera Wang bed topped with Vera Wang sheets and pillows, wearing your Vera Wang nightie. If you have a laptop computer, you can even lie in bed and play the online Vera Wang Resort dress-up fashion game.

clothing. I would not wear that to work, or to a P.T.A. meeting, so where would I wear that?" Other customers loved the fact they could finally afford a designer name and add a bit of flair to their closets.

Vera Wang and Kohl's timed their 2007 launch of Simply Vera perfectly. Over the next two years, the public appetite—and budget—for luxury clothing waned, and designers were forced to drop their prices as an economic recession took hold. The Simply Vera line was an ideal fit for the belt-tightening times.

The Demise of Designer Duds?

As designers presented their spring 2010 collections at Fashion Week in New York City, *The New York Times* called the fall of 2009 "the chilliest retail climate in years ... a difficult moment for high-end fashion."

The recession was clearly taking its toll. People had less money to spend on luxury items—but it was more than the financial downturn that was affecting the fashion industry.

As manufacturers increasingly turned to factories in China that could make their garments at a significantly lower cost, factories in Italy and New York were closing down. Consumers were no longer looking for long-wearing fashion; they wanted cheap chic designed to get them through a season or two before being replaced.

At the high-end department stores, the changing attitude toward luxury clothing—among other expensive products—showed. People were doing less shopping and spending less cash. The stores were losing money and

Vera Wang's Princess line of fragrances was launched in 2006.

Below and right: Creations from the Vera Wang collections at Mercedes-Benz Fashion Week, Bryant Park, New York City, in February 2010. Left: Wearing her own signature attire—a loose-fitting top over black leggings—Vera takes a bow on the runway after her show.

As someone who has combined a lifelong passion for fashion with a remarkable business instinct, this designer-to-the-stars has never been content to sit back and settle down.

began pressuring designers, including Vera Wang, to lower their prices to encourage shoppers to spend.

"In my 40 years in fashion, I've never seen women scared to shop—at all price levels," said Vera, who cut prices for her 2010 resort collection by 40 per cent. "I don't know what's going to happen."

For upscale designers, like Vera, cutting prices might mean more sales, but it can also translate into a damaged reputation. If a Vera Wang dress that usually sells for $1,000, for example, is suddenly offered at $600, a regular customer might question its quality: How can a real Vera Wang dress be selling for just $600? The lower price might also make a wealthy customer feel (gasp!) ordinary, when she is no longer one of the exclusive few who can afford a Vera Wang.

Another factor diluting the high-end fashion biz in the first decade of the 21st century was the trend toward celebrity fashion designers. When celebs first picked up their sketching pencils in the 1980s and 1990s, it wasn't a common phenomenon. By 2009, though, dozens of singers, actors, rappers, models, and athletes called themselves fashion designers, taking away prestige—and dollars—from the Vera Wangs of the world. "Ten years from now, there may be no real designers left," said Vera in 2009.

A Passion for Fashion Forever

Whatever the state of fashion ten years from now, there is no doubt Vera Wang will be in the thick of it, and still a great success, if her

CELEBRITY FASHION DESIGNERS

The world of fashion design isn't limited to, well, fashion designers, any more. Since Jaclyn Smith, who played one of the original *Charlie's Angels*, first launched a clothing line for Kmart in 1985, celebrities have been getting in on the apparel act.

While Smith has sold more than 40 million pieces of clothing in the past quarter century, other star designers are doing just as well. Jennifer Lopez's fashion company, Sweetface, earned $130 million in just one year (2004), and she has since launched a high-end collection of clothing, perfume, and accessories.

Mary-Kate and Ashley Olsen sell toddler, 'tween, and teen clothing as part of their billion-dollar empire. Singer Gwen Stefani has a hit on her hands, bringing in about $90 million a year with her line, called L.A.M.B., first presented in 2004; and rapper/actor/producer Sean "P. Diddy" Combs has made millions on designer duds since he launched his line of men's wear, Sean John, in 1998. In 2004, he earned the CFDA Award for Men's Designer of the Year for his efforts.

Other celebs who have turned their attention to fashion include Sarah Jessica Parker of *Sex and the City* fame, Victoria ("Posh Spice") Beckham, sk8r girl Avril Lavigne, U2 front man and social activist Bono, and pop singer Beyoncé Knowles.

Fashion writers around the world agreed the celebrity-as-designer list hit a low in the fall of 2009 when Lindsay Lohan presented her first fashion line for the House of Emmanuel Ungaro. The line was widely seen as a resounding failure, and Ungaro dropped her before she could create a second one.

business continues to grow at the rate it has for the past two decades. As someone who has combined a lifelong passion for fashion with a remarkable business instinct, this designer-to-the-stars has never been content to sit back and settle down. She has always strived to better herself and her business, just as her parents taught her when she was a little girl. "They fully embraced the American philosophy, [saying] 'This is the land of opportunity. Let's go for it,'" she said—and "go for it" is something Vera continues to do.

"The key is falling in love with something, anything. If your heart's attached to it, then your mind will be attached to it. When you have a passion for something, then you tend not only to be better at it, but you work harder at it too."

Vera Wang

In March of 2010, in the wake of the recession, she boldly opened a massive new boutique in Los Angeles, selling her high-end ready-to-wear in one room, her trademark bridal gowns in another. The same month, she introduced a new fragrance to her Princess line, Glam Princess, bringing her total number of scents to nine for women, one for men.

Throughout her life, whether it's been as an elite, competitive figure skater, as an innovative designer of bridal gowns, or as a businesswoman at the head of a multi-million dollar empire, Vera Wang has always zeroed in on her goals and dreams and pushed herself to achieve them.

What's in Vera Wang's Closet?

Movie stars and presidents' daughters may wear Vera Wang, but Vera Wang doesn't always wear Vera Wang. "No one wears only me. Not even me!" said the designer, who is known to wear incredibly expensive clothing by some of the world's top designers in remarkably random ways. Her favorite look is black leggings under a long, loose top—but the leggings can cost as much as $1,000, and the tops, much, much more.

Among her favorite designers are Miuccia Prada (Italy), Jil Sander (Germany), Yohji Yamamoto (Japan), Louis Vuitton (France), Jean Paul Gaultier (France), Ann Demeulemeester (Belgium), and, of course, her mother's favorite, French designer Yves Saint Laurent.

Sometimes, Vera shops at Kohl's with her daughters but, mostly, she goes for designer outfits and spares no expense to get the best.

"I think I've spent a serious fortune on clothes in my life," said Vera. "I probably could have owned more paintings and sculpture had I not bought all the clothing … It's my passion."

"The key is falling in love with something, anything," she said. "If your heart's attached to it, then your mind will be attached to it. When you have a passion for something, then you tend not only to be better at it, but you work harder at it too."

For Vera, the hard work has paid off. She is acknowledged by fashion insiders as the woman who revolutionized the world of wedding dresses, an innovator who saw an opportunity and leapt at it, changing her own life and the fashion world in the process. With all kinds of markets out there still awaiting her touch, Vera Wang shows no sign of stopping.

Different Season, Different Inspiration

Every Vera Wang collection in every season has a different theme, some obvious, some more subtle. Some of Vera's collections have been inspired by painters, such as French artist Henri Matisse. Sometimes, Vera finds her inspiration in history—ancient Rome or czarist Russia, for example. On occasion, it's a concept like dancewear or the Hollywood red carpet, or maybe she's inspired by a country like Japan. One season, spring 2006, she built a whole collection around the gritty-but-smart TV western series *Deadwood*.

Models display creations from the Vera Wang collections at the February 2010 Mercedes-Benz Fashion Week at Bryant Park in New York City.

Chronology

1949 Vera Ellen Wang is born in New York City on June 27.

1956 Vera's parents give her a pair of ice skates on Christmas Day.

1962 Vera wins her first regional ice skating championship.

1968 Vera is highlighted in the January 8 issue of *Sports Illustrated* magazine in its "Faces in the Crowd" segment, which turns the spotlight on up-and-coming athletes.

1968–1969 Vera and skating partner James Stuart reach the U.S. National Figure Skating Championships. They win fifth place in the junior pairs competition in 1969.

1969 19-year-old Vera abandons her dream of competitive skating. She later drops out of Sarah Lawrence College and moves to Paris to live with French Olympic skater Patrick Pera. She returns to New York and to college within a year.

1970 Vera is hired as a salesperson at the Manhattan Yves Saint Laurent boutique, her first job in the fashion world.

1971 Upon graduation from Sarah Lawrence, Vera is hired as an editorial assistant at *Vogue* magazine.

1972 Vera is promoted to sittings editor, becoming the youngest editor in *Vogue*'s history. She is promoted to senior fashion editor two years later.

1980 Vera meets Arthur Becker for the first time The two date on and off, then break up.

1987 Vera leaves *Vogue* after 16 years and starts a job as design director of accessories at Ralph Lauren. Vera reconnects with Arthur Becker and, this time, they become engaged within a year.

1989 Vera designs her own wedding dress after a frustrating search to find one to buy. On June 22, she marries Arthur Becker. She later quits her job at Ralph Lauren.

1990 Vera opens Vera Wang Bridal House Limited in the Carlyle Hotel in Manhattan.

1991 Vera and Arthur adopt a daughter, Cecilia.

1992 Vera designs costumes for Olympic ice skater Nancy Kerrigan. She designs two more costumes for the skater in 1994.

1994 Vera and Arthur adopt their second child, Josephine. Vera launches an eveningwear line.

1997 Vera teams up with Italian shoe company Rossimoda to create a line of Vera Wang shoes in her first-ever licensing agreement.

1998 In April, Vera stages her first New York fashion show. Vera designs the first Vera Wang Bride Barbie. Another doll in the Designer Barbie series appears a year later, dressed for the red carpet.

2001 Vera publishes *Vera Wang on Weddings.*

2002 On February 14, Vera launches Vera Wang Eau de Parfum at Sak's Fifth Avenue in New York City. The fragrance earns a FiFi Award for best new fragrance. She also launches a line of eyewear, the Vera Wang China and Crystal Collection, and her first-ever ready-to-wear clothing collection.

2003 Vera designs uniforms for the Philadelphia Eagles cheerleading squad. She also launches a jewelry line.

2004 Florence Wang, Vera's mother, dies in January. Vera launches the Vera Wang Silver and Gifts Collection and a new fragrance, Vera Wang for Men.

2005 Vera opens a bridal store in Shanghai, China; wins the CFDA Award for Women's Wear Designer of the Year, and designs the interior of a hotel suite at Halekulani Hotel overlooking Waikiki Beach in Hawaii. In March, her longtime friend and business partner, Chet Hazzard, passes away.

2006 Cheng Ching Wang, Vera's father, dies.

2007 Vera teams up with Kohl's Department Stores and launches a budget clothing line called Simply Vera—Vera Wang.

2009 Vera outfits ice skater Evan Lysacek for the World Championships, later designing his costumes for his gold-medal-winning 2010 Olympic Winter Games performance.

2010 Vera opens her first stand-alone boutique on the West Coast, selling bridal and eveningwear in one shop.

Glossary

boutique A small store that sells fashionable, usually luxury, clothing or other goods

brand name A product made and named by a particular company. Kleenex, for example, is the brand name of a particular facial tissue; Coke is the brand name of a particular cola drink.

brocade A heavy silk, cotton, or woolen fabric with a raised design, often with metallic threads woven through

bustline The part of a woman's garment that lies at the breast or chest

cerebrally Intellectually (as opposed to emotionally)

chic Stylish and modern

compulsively (as in compulsively creative) Having an unstoppable need or urge to do something

democratize To give something popular appeal or to make it accessible to everyone

eau de parfum French term that literally means "perfume water"; a fragrance that isn't as concentrated as "perfume," but is more concentrated than "eau de toilette," in which the aromatic ingredients are more diluted.

elite More talented or more highly trained than other people in the same field or sport

ensemble An outfit consisting of a number of coordinating pieces

Fashion Week A one-week period during which designers show their latest collections in elaborate fashion shows that allow buyers and fashion journalists to see what's hot—and what's not—for the upcoming season

frou-frou Frilly

halter dress A dress that is tied behind the neck, instead of having straps over the shoulders

haute couture French term that literally means "high sewing"; expensive, fancy clothing designed and custom-fit for a specific person

high-end Expensive and luxurious, something likely to appeal to sophisticated people

made-to-order Clothing that is made for a specific person

mainstream Ideas, tastes, or views that are widely accepted in society; not unusual or extreme

mentor A more experienced, usually older, person who teaches and guides a younger, less experienced person, usually related to career direction

pharmaceutical A drug used in medicine

posh Upper-class, elegant, luxurious

prestigious Considered important, impressive, and worthy of respect

ready-to-wear Also called off-the-rack; mass-produced clothing made in standard sizes that will fit most people without much alteration

recession A period of economic slowdown, marked by a decline in household income, personal spending, business profits, and employment; and more bankruptcies and unemployment

savvy A clear and practical understanding of something, based on knowledge, common sense, and good judgment

separates A collection of clothing pieces that can be worn together in various combinations—for example, a set that includes pants, a skirt, a t-shirt, and a blouse

signature (as in *signature fragrance* or *signature style)* A distinctive characteristic that identifies the fragrance or style with a particular individual

sittings editor The person in charge of a magazine's fashion spreads or photo shoots, who decides which model to use, what the model will wear, how he or she will be posed, and where the photo will be shot. The term "sittings" means "photo shoots."

socialite A wealthy person, usually a woman, who is well-known and considered important in upper-class society

stigmatized Denounced or labeled in a scornful way

suite A set of rooms

trade journal A publication dedicated to a particular type of business or industry

trade association An organization dedicated to a particular industry that is funded by its members and works to promote that industry

trademark (as in trademark outfit or trademark hairstyle) A characteristic or attribute associated with a particular person

vintage Involving something made in a previous era and typical of that era. In terms of clothing, vintage is good-quality clothing made between the 1920s and 1980s (anything older is considered antique; anything newer is called contemporary).

Wall Street The street in New York City where many major financial institutions are located

Further Information

Books

Krohn, Katherine. *Biography: Vera Wang*.
Minneapolis, MN: Twenty-First Century Books, 2007.

Krohn, Katherine. *Vera Wang: Enduring Style*.
Minneapolis, MN: Twenty-First Century Books, 2009.

Wang, Vera. *Vera Wang on Weddings*.
New York: HarperCollins, 2001.

Online

WEB SITES:
www.nytimes.com/ref/membercenter/nytarchive.html
This link to *The New York Times* archives is an amazing resource for anyone looking for information on anything that has happened in New York since 1851.

www.evancarmichael.com/Famous-Entrepreneurs/3202/ summary.php
Titled "Famous Entrepreneur Advice," this site provides insights from dozens of successful business people in all different professions and industries. In the "Fashion & Cosmetics" category, for example, 15 entrepreneurs are represented, including Vera Wang. The Vera Wang page then leads to quotes from the designer, motivational advice from her about specific topics, and biographical information.

www.biography.com/articles/Vera-Wang-9542398
This site links to a biography of Vera Wang; the main site, www.biography.com, features more than 25,000 biographies of great lives, past and present, living and dead.

www.asianweek.com/2010/02/09/chinese-american-heroine-vera-wang/#more-11721
AsianWeek, based in San Francisco, is the oldest and largest English-language newspaper serving the Asian/Pacific Islander American community. This site shares profiles of noteworthy Chinese Americans, including Vera Wang.

ONLINE ARTICLES:

Horyn, Cathy. "High Fashion Faces a Redefining Moment," the *New York Times,* September 10, 2009. **http://www.nytimes.com/2009/09/11/style/11fashion.html?_r=1&scp=15&sq=vera+wang&st=nyt**

Larocca, Amy. "Vera Wang's Second Honeymoon," *New York* magazine, January 14, 2006. **http://nymag.com/nymetro/news/people/features/15541/**

Sanz, Cynthia. "Chic to Chic," *People* magazine, July 20, 1998. **http://www.people.com/people/archive/article/0,,20125822,00.html**

Wilson, Eric. "Vera Wang's Business Is No Longer All Dressed in White," *The New York Times,* December 15, 2005. **http://www.nytimes.com/2005/12/15/fashion/thursdaystyles/15VERA.html?scp=1&sq=vera+wang&st=nyt**

Wilson, Eric, and Michael Barbaro. "Can You Be Too Fashionable?" *The New York Times,* June 17, 2007. **http://www.nytimes.com/2007/06/17/business/yourmoney/17vera.html?scp=92&sq=vera+wang&st=nyt**

Witchel, Alex. "From Aisle to Runway; Vera Wang," *The New York Times,* June 19, 1994. **http://www.nytimes.com/1994/06/19/magazine/from-aisle-to-runway-vera-wang.html?pagewanted=1**

DVDs

A Conversation with Vera Wang & Pamela Fiori at Guild Hall. VVH-TV, Hamptons Television, 2009.

Vera Wang: Attention to Detail (DVD). A&E Biography Video, 2001.

Index

About the Author

Diane Dakers was born and raised in Toronto and now makes her home in Victoria, British Columbia. A specialist in Canadian arts and cultural issues, Diane has been a newspaper, magazine, television, and radio journalist since 1991. She loves finding and telling stories about what makes people tick—be they celebrities like Vera Wang, or not-so-famous folks like you and me. Despite a closet full of t-shirts and jeans, Diane has a passion for fashion, and Vera Wang is her all-time favorite designer.